God Wrestler

A poem for every Torah Portion
by Rick Lupert

God Wrestler

Copyright © 2017 by Rick Lupert
All rights reserved

Ain't Got No Press

Layout and Design ~ Rick Lupert
Author Photo ~ Addie Lupert

Many of these poems originally appeared in the "From the Lupertverse" blog at www.JewishJournal.com

This book is protected under the copyright laws of the United States of America. Any reproduction or other unauthorized use of the material or artwork herein is prohibited without the express written permission of the author except in the case of brief quotations embodied in critical articles and reviews.

Second Edition ~ January, 2019

ISBN-13: 978-0-9820584-7-3

Visit the author online at
www.PoetrySuperHighway.com

For bookings, readings, workshops, and incorporating poetry into your community, contact the author at
www.poetrysuperhighway.com/booking

A story that knew but one explanation could hardly be interesting and was certainly not worth the trouble of remembering.

- Chaim Potok

Everything is beautiful, all that matters is to be able to interpret.

- Camille Pissarro

It ain't those parts of the Bible that I can't understand that bother me, it is the parts that I do understand.

- Mark Twain

Thank you Addie, Moses, Adonai, Rabbi David Wolpe, Rabbi Ed Feinstein, Cantor Ellen Dreskin, Yifat Iannaci, all the members of our *first family*, Amy Gross for her invaluable editorial help, and to the Los Angeles Jewish Journal for providing a first home for many of these poems. Thanks to the original author or authors of the Torah...you know who You are. Thanks also to the Hava Nashira community, staff, faculty and participants who never fail to lift me up.

To Addie whose name begins the same way as the transliterated Adonai. There are no coincidences.

בראשת
B'reishit

genesis

B'reishit

In the beginning God made everything.
According to scientists, *the beginning*
took billions of years.

I've taken to counting my ribs.
I want there to be one less so
I have something to believe in.

At the very least
I'm responsible for naming the animals
who live in my house.

I've built a garden in the front
and in the back. I can't eat the fruit
because the possum gets there first.

I call a man in periodically
to keep it looking like paradise.
He brings others to help him.

There are so many more people
eating forbidden fruits
than when all this started.

Noach

It's not a good sign when
already in chapter two
everything gets destroyed.

It's the same way with my son
and the instructions-less *Lego* sets.
He builds and builds

and soon isn't happy with
how it is all going, and then
a flood of disassembled bricks.

He knows no righteous playmate
among playmates. Takes it upon
himself to rebuild

and vocalize the narrative.
He is creator and protagonist.
As far as *two by two* goes

he couldn't be happier.
That's not what the text actually says.
Gathers all twelve of his bears

for the ride.
He'll decide which
gets to be the dove.

Genesis 6:9–11:32

Lech Lecha

Consider the very first Jew – *Abraham*.
Not even his name when the whole thing started.
Had a reputation. The kind of kid

who would destroy the family business.
out of principle. Married the first nice Jewish girl.
Neither of them actually Jewish

when the whole thing started.
The very first converts. Broken idols
noticed by the One who would not be idolized.

The One who gave them the deal of a lifetime.
Go to the shown place. Pack up everything.
No-one likes to move. Something's going to get broken.

Something's going to get lost.
But consider what was gained.
Longer names...holier names...

and a bloodline long enough
to see the whole world still trying
to get to the shown place.

I'd like to trade all my possessions
for the Hebrew letter *hey.*
Pick up extra work as a star in the sky

promised to an ancient ancestor.
That deal you made, *Father Abraham.*
The ink's still drying.

I'm a grain of sand.

Genesis 12:1–17:27

Vayera

I
A child is born.
They name him *laughter.*
Another child is sent away
as if blood doesn't exist.

The original seeds
of a divided Jerusalem
are sown right here.
Hardly anyone laughs there now.

II
Every day Sodom and Gomorrah
happen in front of my house.
I'm taking a census of the righteous

in my neighborhood.
I'm having trouble getting to the number one.
I want the police to take them away

their trash too.
We could use a localized gentrification.
A pillar of salt.

III
Despite my son's worst behavior
I don't think I could take him to the rock
no matter Who asked.

Abraham should have argued.
He was already famous for that.
Nothing to prove.

Let us make a covenant with life.
Reserve salt, only for our tongues.
Open the tent to all our children.

Chayei Sarah

I
What is it with this this mortal impermanence?
You live and do things and the end is inevitable.

Like a story called *life* which begins with a death.
A reminder all our narratives have the same end game.

On the same day as a Syracuse mother's yahrzeit.
On the same day that a Van Nuys wife

travels to Pennsylvania to bury her grandmother.
We don't live into our hundreds like our founding parents.

But ninety-four is pretty good.
Let's all live to ninety-four.

II
It used to be you could travel to your uncle's house
and marry the first girl you found at the well.

So what if you had the same grandfather.
There were limited options and, back then,

population explosion wasn't even a thing.
There is value in water, and a woman who brings it

is a giver of life. Always marry a woman who gives you water,
who tends to your camels without having been asked.

III
Oh California, you are so thirsty.
I had to travel to Wisconsin just to have a drink.

My well is still there, though I brought my Rebekah home.
Her name is spelled and pronounced differently in this world.

But I am never without a soothing beverage.
Even as Sarah is laid into the ground.

Dig deeper California. Separate the salt from the ocean.
May we live on your ground as long as our matriarchs.

Toledot

Jacob and Esau
fighting in the womb
like kittens

one escapes, the other
hanging on by a foot.
Our first family

ladies and gentleman.
One grows hair while
their father grows blind.

One more interested
in sports on TV
than birthright

or inheritance.
Sells the whole thing
to the smooth skinned

slick talker for
a bowl of soup.
Mom set it up!

Our first family
ladies and gentleman!
Off to separate

corners, they go.
One to the desert.
One to the gentrified 'hood

of Uncle Laban.
The source of all
Jewish wives.

I'd tell you what happened
but there's a sequel
in the works.

That's how they
keep you coming back.
Our first family

ladies and gentleman!
They're coming to your town
They'll work in your fields

They'll marry your daughters.
But that's a story for
another week.

Advanced tickets
on sale now. Hang on
to your brothers foot.

Vayetzei

I
It's getting so all my poems about the Torah
read like a *JDate* ad campaign run by old Uncle Laban
Jacob, two wives and their handmaidens later

and suddenly a *baker's dozen* of children
running around the campground
like *they own the place.*

My wife and I had the good sense to stop at one.
At least that was my idea; she would have gone on forever.

But thirteen children in the Land of Canaan!
Can you imagine the diaper situation?
We definitely would have used a service.

Despite the obvious allure of gifted sheep
Jacob can't *shake the feeling*
There's no place like home.

Steals away with his family...
with *our* family
with the stealth of billion dollar technology.

Sets up shop in the Holy Land
where angels meet them
like old neighbors bearing fruit.

II
Two Dreams

Old Uncle Laban
with the sand of night
in his eyes
lets Jacob
go.

Jacob
a stone for a pillow
a ladder to the sky

*like we all haven't found
construction materials
in the desert*

wrestles with himself
at the cornerstone
of a Holy Land,

takes the name *Israel,*
gives it to all of us.

Vayishlach

Somewhere along the Jabbok River
which has a different name if you come
from the other side of the family

Jacob leaves half *his* family
to meet his long-lost brother
from whom he'd taken everything.

Somewhere along the river
a wrestling match occurs.
Team Jacob versus team unknown man.

Team unknown man's
only advantage, besides anonymity,
is pressure against Jacob's thigh.

A pain he would feel for days.
A familial pain we still feel when
the heart is not tended to.

Thousands of years later
it is Thanksgiving in Pennsylvania.
Two cousins wrestle in front of a football game.

Team seven year old
versus team a year and a half.
They both hold their own.

No river between them.
One carries the other into
the room with the big people.

Nothing but smiles.
Back in history Jacob takes on a new name
is kissed by his long-lost brother

despite the incidents with the soup
and the fake hair, in which
everything was taken.

A matriarch and a patriarch pass away.
Even our first family is impermanent,
is subject to burial on the side of the road.

Somewhere along the Jabbok River
brothers are always brothers
no matter which bank they walk along

No matter
what tongue they use
to say its name.

Vayeishev

Everything I learned about the story of Joseph
I learned from the musical.

I can't think about his adventures without the voice
of the narrator telling it to us in rhyme.

I can't think about the Butler Joseph meets in Egypt Jail
without Joseph telling him he will *live to 'butle' again.*

Not in the original text but that's how Andrew Lloyd Weber
and Tim Rice told it to me, interpreting the Torah

like any troupe of musical Chasids,
making it rock and roll to bring it home for a rock and roll era.

The twelve sons of Jacob, who became French in
one scene for some reason; I don't know how Jacob

had thirteen children, I can barely have one without wanting to
throw him in a pit, sell him to a passing band of Ishmaelites.

I guess despite the obvious he's still my favorite.
We ply him with the multi-colored coats of our day.

Video games and Barbies for God's sake.
Maybe that's why we don't have more.

So there's nothing to be jealous of.
So we'll never see a bloodied garment

accompanied by tales of devouring beasts.
Beware in Egypt my son. You're attractive enough

to raise the eyebrows of all the Mrs. Potiphars.
You may be running the place some day,

but, remember, it's not all about you.
Don't forget about us in the Van Nuys of Canaan.

A famine is coming and whatever wheat is today
we're going to need that.

Those Canaan days. They grow up so quickly.
It's like a dream.

Miketz (or How the Wheat Was Won)

If there ever was a series of Torah Portions
worthy of binge-studying, this is it.

Cliffhanger after cliffhanger - The Story of Joseph: Episode 2.
Our hero in jail, where we left him last week.

Still scarred from the pit, his best friend, the butler, gone.
Things aren't looking great – It's a real page-scroller.

Our new antagonist, Pharaoh, it's like an origins story,
not such a bad guy at this point.

But he's the pod-racing young Anakin Skywalker
to his Vader-like descendants.

It's gonna be trouble, right here in Egypt city.
He's dreaming of cows.

Joseph, still in jail, still wearing the pajamas
of the house of Potiphar, happens to be an expert

in dreams about cows, saves the day! Wheat for everyone!
Pharaoh, like an Emperor Palpatine, no-one yet suspects

gives Joseph the keys to the Kingdom.
Joseph, in one of the best relationship plot twists

since his dad married the wrong woman,
marries the daughter of the woman who accused him of rape.

Soon little Josephs running around the kingdom,
and Mrs. Potiphar can't say a thing.

And this is where the writers
(or *writer* if you believe such things)

make their money, focusing on character development.
Joseph's brothers, in search of Egypt wheat

find themselves bowing in front of a man
they do not know they know.

The youngest, accused of stealing a silver goblet
and the credits roll, another cliffhanger.

That's how they keep you coming back.
You only have to wait 'til next week.

You might remember the outcome from last season.
We do this every year. But no spoilers please.

For some people
it's their very first time.

Vayigash

Like Joseph, I know what it's like to
not have a father for decades.

Mine, hidden in the Egypt of Texas
pretending he was someone else

while I built my empire in
the land of California.

Like Joseph's brothers, it was me
who showed up on his doorstep.

But I knew exactly who he was.
Unlike the brothers, I wasn't there for wheat

or even fancy coats. I just wanted to make sure
the space between us would

no longer be measured in decades.
A cautionary lunch ensued

and then he brought me my sister
like Benjamin, only, a girl.

America became our land of Goshen
and we continue to flourish.

Like the familial bond between Joseph
and his brothers, there is nothing to forgive.

We didn't move to Texas, of course
the Egypt of our story.

I read ahead in the text and
it turns out things go south down there.

No-one wants to move twice.
But there is an airplane ticket in the future.

Next week, in fact. Round trip.
The first family lives on.

Vayechi

I revel in the fake spoiler.
We can't start a single episode
of any television show without
me turning to my wife and
telling her

*This is the episode where
everyone dies.*

So I hope I'm not giving
too much away when I tell you
this is the last you'll see of
our first family.

Jacob, the final patriarch
dead and buried in the Holy Land.
Egyptians accompany Jacob's burial party.

*Can you imagine how quickly
war would end if we went
to the funerals of our enemies?*

Joseph, the dream catcher
dead and not yet buried
in the Holy Land until his body's
cameo in the next book.

And like any good ending
the fate of all the characters is revealed.
Judah will make leaders
Levi scholars
Issachar seafarers
Dan will grow olives.

Everybody has a part to play.
Even the step children are blessed.

A little bit of the magic leaves too.
Jacob wants to tell his sons
the secret of the end of days.
But at exactly that moment
the Divine Spark vacates the premises.

You can't give away all the secrets
or no-one will watch the sequel.
This franchise has legs and
some things have yet to be written.

*Be strong, be strong
and we will be strengthened.*

שמות
Sh'mot

exodus

Shemot

I

A new King rose over Egypt who did not know Joseph.

It is in our nature to be fruitful and multiply.
To grow strong when left alone.
To win Nobel prizes and invent technology

that turns salt into sweet.
So, centuries into our stay in the narrow place
it is no surprise the locals became nervous.

It may be the first time the Israelites
are referred to as a problem.
But it won't be the last.

II

Every son who is born you shall cast into the Nile

This is where the idea of
the strong woman was invented.

Shifrah and Pooah,
the midwives who refused to

follow Pharaoh's instructions,
who let the boys live.

Yocheved, who floated her son
down the river to save him from those

who would put him
in the river.

Miriam who followed a waterproof basket
who tricked a princess into

letting a baby return to
his mother.

Pharaoh's daughter
who doesn't get a name

who defied her father
and raised a Hebrew child

as her own.
This is where the idea of

the strong woman was invented.
There would be no Moses

without them.

III

Behold the bush was burning, but not consumed

Enter the reluctant hero
Shoes off and having a conversation with the Lord
Speech impediment and all.

Armed with miracles and
a well spoken brother.
Did I mention the fancy stick?

You're not going to impress anyone
without a fancy stick.
Takes a meeting with the Pharaoh.

Tells him *we're Milk and Honey bound.*
Doesn't go well. Now the people
have to make bricks out of nothing.

The first reported case of kvetching
happens right here.
Pharaoh snickering in one corner.

Moses, the referee.
The Lord on the other side of the ring
dancing like a prize fighter

who hasn't even started yet.

Va'eira

I'm gonna harden my heart
I'm gonna swallow my tears
I'm gonna turn and leave you here

~ Quarterflash

If you like miracles
tangible evidence of the supernatural

than this is the Torah portion for you.
It really gets going. Sticks turned to snakes

rivers turned to blood.
Frogs, falling out of the sky!

The people who thought up umbrellas
never dreamed of this.

It's raining amphibians
for God's sake!

And the man holding the purse strings
hardens his heart every time.

We beg for our lives when
the danger is in our face.

And when it's gone
we act like it doesn't smell of rotting frogs.

What are twenty first century plagues?
Guns raining out of the sky

into the hands of people who
don't believe in magic.

The president, a Moses
tries to make them go away.

Ridiculed by those who've
never heard of the promised land.

People living under the freeway
a modern day Goshen.

Ignored by golden Egyptians
our hearts hardened as we drive on by.

This isn't over.
A stick is raised in the air.

It's an El Niño year.
The worst is yet to come.

Bo

I

Locusts

A few months after we moved into our house
the ants felt bold enough to join us.

Their line from the back door to
the trash can, a plague that inspired us

to hire a monthly pest-control service.
We were like modern day Pharaohs

ignoring the miracles of the wilderness
in our quest to build a treasure city

in the heart of Van Nuys.
We haven't seen them since.

But soon after the meal worms came, and
we had to learn to shut the front door quickly

so the moths, attracted to our light
wouldn't join our inside festivities.

You can build a home in the desert.
But the desert will never let you forget

what you did.

II

Darkness

It's not like turning out the lights
or the altogether absence of electricity.

Or being in the wilderness where
the light of long dead stars

creates a natural majesty.
It is thick. It is palpable.

You can feel the nothing
with your eyes.

Even your torches
reveal only more nothing.

That is the darkness that came.
That is the darkness you never want.

Not even to sleep by.
A living death.

Nothing to see here.

III

Slaying of the First Born

You'd think, after the river turned to blood
after the cattle death, and

the wild beasts walking down Main Street
Pharaoh might have gotten the message.

After the frogs and the realization that
you can't find a good skin doctor in Egypt.

The locusts, the darkness, should have
been enough to soften a heart.

I know if someone told me it was
find a new staff or my son would die

I'd be on *Craig's List,* faster than you
could say *Help Wanted.*

It's a stupid man who outlives his son,
who finds his kingdom filled only with

empty neighborhoods,
who hears the cries of the departing

Better get used to flat bread.
That's all the time we have.

Beshalach

Do you remember what it was like?
Walls of water taller than a Grand Canyon.

Our feet on dry land.
I have a vague memory of even the mud

being dry, so the walk was comfortable.
Is that how you remember it?

What about stepping up on the other side
only to see chariots in the distance?

The brief fear that it was all a lie
that we can't really have nice things

assuaged by the closing water
and the floating spears.

A song and dance led by a sister
the one who followed the basket

a sweet singer of Israel.
Do you remember that melody?

It was us, after all,
not a separate set of people

thousands of years ago.
Those were our feet.

Those were our voices.
Do you still sing of your own freedom?

Can you find the double portions of manna
laid out for you as you take your left turns?

The water springing from your rocks.
Are your feet still dry?

I sing a song of the sea.
I remember it like it was yesterday.

Yitro

I
Autocorrect wanted to change
the title of this poem, from *Yitro* to *Nitro*.

I almost didn't change it back.
God, after all, descends from the mountain

amidst thunder, lightning and smoke.
Like a super-hero named *Nitro*.

Like Stan Lee dreamed up the whole thing.
Only instead of the awe one would expect

when one costumed in fire comes to
stop the robbery, get the cat out of the tree

and generally save the day, the people
are scared out of their Egyptian pajamas.

Beg Moses to do all the talking.
We love our fantasies on paper

and digital screens. But
I guess we should leave them there.

When buildings really start to come down
we'll *blockbust* our way home

so fast.

II
The people arrive at the mountain of all mountains.
Seven weeks in to feeling pretty good about

their triumph in the narrow place.
Enter the father in law with familial advice

Trumped by the Father of all laws
and a famous list of ten,

the original historical document.
I take one, one, one 'cause there is something

bigger than you. Wear a reminder on your head
and don't forget.

and two, two, two because you're worshiping
an idol right now. Stop it.

and three, three, three because words hurt
so take care before they spill out of your mouth.

and four, four, four 'cause everybody
needs a vacation, even just a day once a week.

and five five, five for your mother and father
who, despite how you felt about them as a teenager

made it so you existed at all.
and six, six, six 'cause all we have is life

and if you take a life, you've taken everything.
and seven, seven 'cause she is the

other half of you, one soul, one flesh.
and eight, eight I forget that what I have is enough.

and nine, nine, nine for a lost truth
and the damage it causes.

and ten, ten, ten, ten for everything, everything
everything I already have in my own house.

It's all I need.

Mishpatim

Do not cook a kid in its mother's milk.
                               Exodus 23:19

I became a vegetarian spontaneously one day
in an *Islands* restaurant after reading a pamphlet
from a pen-pal about vivisection.

It was 1986, back when having a pen-pal was a thing.
I was eighteen years old and, as is the custom
of that age, I knew everything there was to know.

That was my last chicken sandwich, or anything, really,
that had a face. Unless you count the beef I accidentally
ate last year when *Chipotle* got my order wrong.

Thirty years later, animals with sacred faces
roam my Van Nuys halls. I wouldn't cook them
in anything, let alone their mother's milk.

Other creatures, like foreigners, have found their way
to my front door, and I, fueled by the memory of
being a stranger in Egypt, open my tent to them,

lay out plastic bowls of premium food
so they will feel whole. So the human family
expands beyond its artificial boundaries.

Attention politicians: It says in the oldest texts
to welcome the stranger, not pretend the lines
we have drawn are not abhorrent to nature.

Take heed as you appeal for our votes.
A human being is a human being, even if they're
from New Jersey, or places even stranger.

My conscience sits on my lap every day.
We are the consuming fire. We are forty days
and forty nights. These are the laws we live by.

Terumah

*They shall make for Me a Sanctuary,
and I shall dwell amidst them.*
                              Exodus 25:8

Imagine going to Ikea
and only buying the instructions.

The materials themselves come
from what you brought out of Egypt,

from what your heart
inspires you to give.

And it ain't gonna be cheap!
Everything plated in gold!

Do you know how expensive
acacia wood is?

What are cubits anyway?
Is that metric?

To make a holy space
we must give the best we have.

We must create with
an artist's sensibility

and a craftsman's hands.
This thing we build

has to last decades
in the desert.

And in the end, the final product
is lost to history except

in famous movies and
ancient descriptions.

You can make any place
into a sacred space.

But if you want the Holy One
to dwell in your new cabinets

it's gonna cost ya.
Be an artist.

Don't skimp on materials.
And generations later

they'll watch movies about
what you made.

Tetzaveh

My mother was a Cohen and so
as far as I know, I'm descended from Aaron
and have *priest* running through my veins.

After reading the description of
what they had to wear, I'm not sure
how long I would have lasted in the job.

I don't own a tie.
I remember leaving a job at a new organization
shortly after they announced everyone

would have to wear a uniform.
When my wife asks what I'm going to wear
to an event of some kind

I mumble something about the sky
and then get out of that conversation
as fast as I can.

I suspect it may be a front.
I'm maddeningly specific about
how I want my t-shirts to fit.

Addie begs that I buy a second pair
of jeans, so that when the ones I wear
every day, all day, forever, wear out

there won't be a crisis of faith.
And the stones silk-screened on my shirts
Star (Wars and Trek), Zeppelin (Led)

and the Beastie Boys (all three nice Jewish boys).
They decorate my *Breastplate of Judgement*
like tribes. I'm the high priest of my own special world.

One more thing; God is a meat-eater.
Asks for two lambs a day, one on the morning,
one in the afternoon.

Promises to dwell amongst us.
Maybe this is why I have trouble finding Him/Her.
I'm a vegetarian.

I don't know if the Holy One
would like vegan lamb samosas.
I'd like to find out, though.

Ki Tisa

Steps to a successful covenant:

I
Get the people involved.
A monetary investment will create
a sense of ownership.
A half shekel should do it.
But don't give them grief if
they can't pay. There is no
source of income in the desert.

II
Use local artisans.
Anyone can make a box, a square,
a portable room. But if you want to make
a normal space sacred. you'll need an
artist's sensibility. See if Bezalel is available.
He does good work
and is reasonable.

III
Make sure they include the practicals.
So much illness could be prevented
if we just remembered to wash our hands.

IV
Don't succumb to impatience.
Impatience will lead to you
melting down your family jewelry.
You'll start to mold it into animal shapes
like a panda, or a calf even.
Try to remember the panda's eyes
are just your aunt Gertie's wedding ring
and not a sign of true divinity.

V
If your leader comes down the mountain
a day or two later than expected
don't freak out. There was probably traffic
or the meeting ran long. If he throws
the tablets at you, you probably
ignored section IV.

VI
When your leader comes down the mountain
again, tells you he just successfully argued
against your complete annihilation,
believe him. The beams of light projecting
off his face are a sign he's telling the truth.

VII
A few quick reminders: Don't melt anything
into the shape of anything else (again.) And
definitely don't worship it if you do.
Out of respect for mothers everywhere,
don't mix milk and meat. Here's a little secret:
all mammals are lactose intolerant after
they're weaned from their mothers. I'm
serious about this.

VIII
Take a day off. Every week.
You won't find the Holy One dwelling amongst
you if you're still checking your email
on Saturday. But if you turn it off
let the day of rest envelop you
you'll find They were right there all along
right where They promised to be.

Vayakhel

I didn't want to write another poem
about the building of the Tabernacle

but as with any new construction
the project is running long.

Or maybe we were just talking
about it all these weeks and now

after all the instructions have been repeated
and all the permits have been pulled

the work is finally happening.
The people are into it.

Giving far more materials
than are required to get the job done.

When does that happen?
A budget running *under*.

This is the kind of micromanaging
that could really make a difference.

We should make someone from
this story President of the World.

The Tabernacle, an ancient White House
for our elected leader to dwell amongst us.

We did choose this, right?
Or were we the ones chosen?

I'm going to give generously
to the point where they have to

tell me to stop. So there's no worry
about the project getting done.

I'm going to take a day off.
That's what they keep reminding me to do.

An instruction I expect to be repeated
for many weeks to come.

Pekudei

Guess who's coming to dinner?
Let's skip to the end, I'll tell you.
It's a Cloud.

A Cloud is coming to dinner.
The Cloud knows we've
made all the sacred outfits.

Even the reversed apron.
What a genius idea, a reversed apron
so food doesn't stain the design.

Of course, you may have to
bake backwards. I'm sure there are
diagrams for this on the way.

It's nothing but instructions until
we are strong, and strong and strengthened.
It's all being assembled now.

Moses himself is installing the
screen door. People are sprinkling oil
on all the pieces.

As the Italians say,
it's not official until we
sprinkle oil on it.

Let's get it all in place
before the Cloud comes.
Actually, the Cloud won't come

until it's all in place.
That's the point of all these instructions.
We're Cloud-proofing the joint.

It's all very exciting but
no one realizes this dinner party
will last for forty years.

Time enough for a
generation of *anointers* to
pass into the desert sand.

Time enough for us
to deserve to get where we're going.
That Cloud is going to stick with us

well past dessert. There's nothing
like a good meal to make us feel
strong and strengthened.

ויקרא
Vayikra

leviticus

Vayikra

The man who has a conscience suffers
whilst acknowledging his sin. That is his punishment.

— Fyodor Dostoyevsky, Crime and Punishment

I
Olah - The Ascending Offering

We start with the hardest one.
Let the people know what they're in for
before you lighten up with food.

I think it was the
voices in Ralph Wiggum's head
that said "Burn Everything".

And so everything is burned.
Every piece of the animal.
Nothing left

but smoke
a *pleasing fragrance to the Lord*
a fan of barbecue, no doubt.

When we give away
something expensive
we all go up.

II
Minchah - The Meal Offering

This is where the Italians
got the idea for focaccia
unleavened bread

drizzled in oil. You can see
where we're going with this.
The Lord was the first one

to emphasize the importance
of seasoning your food.
Salt with salt, God says

as if one could salt
with anything else.
Don't forget the salt

God goes on
in the very same sentence.
No wonder it took

forty years to get somewhere
with so much time spent
on these details.

III
Shelamim - The Peace Offering

The instructions for the
peace offering read like
an episode of **Hannibal**.

The word *blood* already in
verse two, then three more times
before we move on.

Mentions of kidneys
and innards and the fat that
surrounds them.

The liver makes an appearance.
Who knew they were already
concerned with the names

of internal organs
back before history
could be proven.

It seems peace
always begins
with death.

IV
Chatat - The Sin Offering

Justice is delivered
on a sliding scale.
The wealthy

gave a sheep or goat.
A person of lesser means
only two birds.

A pauper, required
to bring a meal. (Hopefully
they didn't forget the salt.)

This was the first flat tax.
People required to give
what they could

no concern at all
paid to the sin
they committed.

V
Asham - The Guilt Offering

Have you ever
crossed a line you
didn't know was there

only to find yourself
on the other side, surprised
by the wreckage?

Isn't it true it is only
every *other* driver who is the pagan?
Until you veer into their

lane, with a wave
of acknowledgement
trying to communicate

that's not who I am.
We are all unintentionally guilty.
Prepare your kidneys

the Lord is hungry.

Tzav

So, you want to be a priest.
Or maybe you were just born into it.

Either way, the details rival any
fraternity or sorority initiation.

I only mention *sorority* because
of my egalitarian sensibility.

We all know at Mount Sinai women
were not part of the hazing rituals.

So, you want to be a priest.
Well get this, right away we learn

*and he shall don his linen
trousers on his flesh.*

From the get-go Judaism mandates
wearing pants. And it's so specific.

You can't just have your pants with you.
You need to, literally, put them on your body.

So, you want to be a priest. Hey, that's
okay, but pretty soon in you're told

*and he shall take off his garments
and put on other garments.*

And now you're left thinking you
need a wardrobe budget if you're

going to take this job. And you don't
have a choice but to take this job

because you're a Cohen and
that's the family business.

So, you want to be a priest.
And they try to distract you from

all the details of pants, and
putting on other clothes by telling you

And the fire on the altar shall burn on it;
it shall not go out.

And I guess it wasn't Morrissey who
first said *there is a light that never goes out.*

And I'm pretty sure that Morrissey wears pants
which makes me believe in him all the more.

So, you want to be a priest.
And it starts to get a little crazy

up in this Tabernacle when Moses
starts sprinkling oil and blood

on all the initiates.
And they're told

And you shall not leave the entrance of
the Tent of Meeting for seven days

and seven days is a long time
to stand anywhere,

wearing the same pants
covered in oil and blood

eating the gifted flesh
tending to the flame.

Shemini

I
and the glory of God appeared to all the people.
                    Leviticus 9:23

And who wouldn't want to bring
a housewarming gift to Israel's newest resident?
God is coming to the Tabernacle.

And it's not just a *stop-by*.
He's moving in (or *she* if you prefer.)
So before you show up to welcome the One

to the neighborhood, stop by the florist,
or perhaps the Kosher butcher, as God
is a big fan of animal parts – innards

fat and blood. Or maybe make a trip to
Venice Beach where they sell a million kinds
of incense at tables that stretch for miles.

But make sure to only buy from
incense sellers with a Heschsher
as the wrong kind of incense

will get you burst into flames.
Just ask Aaron's sons Nadab and Abihu
who no longer exist.

II
*These are the creatures that you may eat
among all the animals on earth*
                    Leviticus 11:2

Newsflash: Some insects are Kosher
including four different types of locusts!
Lookout Oaxacan, Kosher is coming for you.

This is the dinner party you'll
never attend in Pico Robertson.
Brooklyn, *maybe*.

This is the dinner party the
Jewish survivalists have been waiting for!
Jiminy Cricket,

I'm so sorry,
you're on the menu!
Flipper gets a reprieve.

I remember once my mother
tried to feed me dolphin.
We were living in Florida and

Flipper was still on the TV.
This is the same woman who
made me go to Hebrew School.

I refused to eat it.
How could I know she was just
doing the work of the *Lord*?

III
My mother, like God
despite my resistance
a consistent presence
in my tent.

Tazria

I know the newborn kittens, living on my front porch
aren't Jewish. But they are under my care, and I'm
having trouble telling their mother that as a result

of bringing these beauties into the world, that she
is unclean. I know the newborn kittens living on
my front porch, and their mother, aren't human,

but I'm relying on our bond as fellow mammals
to help me through this instruction, that once you do
the holiest thing you can do, bring a life into the world

that you are somehow tainted...that you need to be
separated. That *therefore choose life* comes with
the fine print of *Mikveh required*.

Thank you, Torah, for giving me the comfort that if
Kaiser is one day closed when an unknown skin
condition surfaces on my body, that I can turn to you

for instructions on how to remove myself from society.
Thank you Torah, for the medical training you gave
the priestly class, so I can know just how long I

should be gone. Thank you Torah, for the reminder
of my circumcision. I've been trying to forget about it
for decades, but every year, already in verse three, you

bring up that particular covenant, and the *enchsnippening*
of my past displays on my internal screen like
YouTube clips of classic movies. I know they had color

in 1968, but as is the custom with nostalgia, this
is in glorious black and white. Couldn't You, God Almighty,
with all Your supernatural technology, have created us

without the need to offer a tip, so soon in? And don't think,
Torah, I missed your note on burning my clothing.
I'm kind of with you on this one. I've been considering

burning my pants since the mid-nineties. Hardly five
minutes of any conversation goes by without me
suggesting "Hey. Should we burn all our clothing?

Let's start with our pants." And hello, reader, I know
you're there. Are you having trouble with all of this?
My separation anxiety assessment? Me too!

I embrace the concept of the one tent, and when the
instructions say some people can't be in the tent
my inclusive feathers get ruffled.

I'm going to give this a break and head to the front porch.
I want to be showered in newborn kittens.
Nothing would make me feel cleaner.

Metzora

Two live birds, a cedar stick, a strip of crimson, and hyssop.
(I'll give you a minute to look up "hyssop"...still here? OK
it's a plant.) Sounds like *Better Homes and Gardens gone wild.*

Parents: you may want to send the children into the other room.
Not indoors? Have them commingle in the hyssop shrubbery.
(Once you use a word twice, you own it.)

Let's cut to the chase: One of the birds isn't going to make it,
and after all the slaughtering and the dipping and, I'm really
not sure what's happening with the cedar plank, but

all of this is leading to you being purified. Did I mention
you're going to have to shave off all your hair? My *Adonai!*
If that happened to me, we'd be here 'til the end of Deuteronomy.

The priestly class would be growing entire beards while I
painstakingly shaved mine off. Please don't picture this.
Please don't picture any of this. If you're *the children,*

why on Earth are you reading this and not frolicking
amongst the hyssop? For the love of *Yud Hey Vav Hey*
don't, under any circumstances, read chapters fifteen on.

There are certain things you don't need to know about.
Not yet anyway. But take comfort knowing the Torah
covers every possible circumstance. Every bit of knowledge

you will need is in there. You'll know what to do when
lesions appear on your house. You'll know what to do
when they migrate to your clothes. You'll know what to do

when it reaches your skin. The birds, the stick, the crimson,
the hyssop. Now's a good time to put in a ritual jacuzzi.
You've got immersing to do. But don't forget what

got you here. A slip of the tongue. A mistranslated word.
An evil sentiment voiced against another. This is the
kind of thing that can get your house purified out

of existence. This is why the gas leaks come. This is why
the pipes sometimes break. This is why every person you meet,
despite their appearance, should be treated like a goldmine

of possibility. You are the living bird. You are the spring water.
You are the fields of hyssop along the Mediterranean coast.
If you can use the word hyssop seven times in a single poem

you can do anything.

Acharei Mot

It's amazing we invented the concept
of the scapegoat, only to have it used against us
during the second war to end all wars.

And one can't help but feel bad for the goat
both of them really. One to be sacrificed
the other to be sent off into the desert.

Who decides?
What did either of these goats do?
What did any of us do?

And then there's the story of the holiest
spot there is, and most of us can never go there.
Just the one person, on the one day,

dressed in white
(don't worry, it's ages before Labor Day)
enters through a cloud of smoke.

Apologizes for everything everyone has done.
It's the ultimate backstage pass.
I guess if someone is willing to

take responsibility for all my sins
I'll find other places to be holy.
I think it was Han Solo who

famously said "It's not my fault."
Honestly, I have nothing else to say about that
I just think it's important to mention

Han Solo periodically.
And speaking of famous people.
This is the parsha that proves definitively

that Dracula could not be Jewish.
Don't drink blood. Cover it with dust.
I'm sorry, Vlad, you are not one of us.

And if you ever needed a list of
who not to sleep with, or more specifically
whose nakedness not to uncover

may I suggest Leviticus chapter 18?
This is the one that fuels the fire of the
homophobes. But the text isn't as specific

as they would have you believe.
Let's eliminate the prefixes from the word
leaving only *sexuality*.

I took French in high school
where the word *mot* means "word."
Here it means "death."

Sometimes I
just want to be
in Paris.

Kedoshim

And you shall be holy, because I am holy.
And the laundry list of obligations begins.

> *Fear your mother and father.*

I wish I'd learned about this earlier.
I was never afraid of my parents
although one of them is much taller than me.
He travels undefeated in every circle.
It would be reasonable to be cautious but
instead we developed a camaraderie.
I'm teaching my son the same.

And you shall be holy, because I am holy.
I'd say I wish there was an instruction manual
but this *is* the instruction manual.

> *You shall not collect the fallen individual grapes*
> *of your vineyard. You shall leave them for the poor.*

And I wonder if the old possum who's lived here
longer than us counts as *the poor*. I caught him
in our almond tree and soon there were no almonds.
We haven't seen peaches grow to their fruition in years.
Meanwhile the homeless build camps under
freeway overpasses blocks away, and our
neighborhood gathers their pitchforks.
Why is the animal innocent and the human
animal a scourge?

And you shall be holy, because I am holy.
This is the citizenship test of mother earth.

> *When you plant a tree, you shall not
> eat its fruit for three years.*

I wish they'd told me this when we planted our
pomegranate tree a few months ago.
We expected to be counting the seeds for
the new year, but now our son will have met
double digits before that sweetness meets our tongues.
We're not sure why they planted a dwarf sized tree either.
But it is in the ground now and this is a lifelong commitment.

And you shall be holy because I am holy.
This whole thing is a lifelong commitment.

> *You shall observe My Sabbath.*

This isn't the first time this has been mentioned
and, I've read ahead, it won't be the last.
Six days is pretty impressive to make a world
and in the end it wasn't us who did the work.
So out of deference to the enormity of the project
take a break. This is the ultimate *Miller Time*.
Or whatever craft brew you prefer. Or maybe
you're an abstainer. That's the point, abstain,
at least for a day, at least every week.

And you shall be holy, because I am holy.
This is the stuff that puts marrow in your bones.

Emor

My mother's maiden name was Cohen
but because the blood of this tradition
only runs through the veins of our fathers
she was not entitled to anything special.

She wouldn't believe that if you told her,
though, and I can recount a lifetime of
occasions where she was convinced
she was related to the kings and queens

of the world. There was an almost daily
check of the mailbox for the *royalty* check
which never came. I only recently learned
of the patrilineal entitlements of our priestly

class. It's not that I made a point to avoid
cemeteries. To my knowledge I've never
interacted with a human corpse, though I
do enjoy the zombie-centric television shows

which are the fashion of our day. It's a relief
to know I'm not bound by the restrictions or
entitlements of the sons of Aaron. Though
the other six hundred plus laws are waiting

for their turn on my mantle. At least there are
my cousins, the three Cohen boys, all of
whom erect Christmas trees without the
weight of history telling them otherwise.

I don't mean to act like a Hollywood name-
dropper but I know I could ask them for holy
favors if I needed to. One of them bought me
shoes once. Another took a dessert sampler

platter for the cause. The third transports
our child, from state to state so my wife and I
can periodically leave the continent. Their
father, the big Cohen, has a heart larger than

the second Temple. Speaks and eats Yiddish
like a habit. These are the priests in my life.
The holiest men I know. They've built me
a bridge to thirty five hundred years ago.

Forgive the round number.
We interpret as we go.

Behar

If you were the earth
out of which everyone's food grew
animal and human alike

you would need a rest too.
You *need* a rest too. Take one.
Not in seven years.

Every year, a week or two
outside of your element. It will
help *define* your element.

Every week, a full day.
We keep repeating this
until the time between

instances of *that day* diminishes
and someone does drink from the
extra cup at the table.

Every day, a full hour
or, do like the Spanish and
take a siesta, a day off

in the middle of your day.
And what are you doing at night?
I hope not thinking about the day.

The two are different.
That's in chapter one. You
may have to start this

over if you missed that.
Give it a few months and you
will start this over.

When the leaves leave
the trees. When the heat of your
summer rest is reduced to

digital memories. When
the round keeps coming around
and the slaves are freed

and the complicated laws of
real estate find their ancient roots.
Take a rest. We are not

the owners here. It would be
generous to call us the caretakers.
Take a rest. Free your slave.

Put your food in the cabinet
for later. This is the Earth. Giver
of all, to all. Goodnight Earth.

Bechukotai

It takes twenty verses or so to tell us of all
the blessings we'll earn if we follow the rules.

It seems like a lot until you see the forty
or so that follow, telling us of all the curses

we'll suffer, if we don't. Shouldn't it be the
other way around? I don't tell my son I

will chastise him for eternity if he doesn't
brush his teeth. I might take story away for

one night. Possibly deny him a dessert-based
snack. But that's the extent of it. I don't

mean to criticize the author, or the authors or
the rule makers, or the interpreters of the

ancient rules…I mean, I need to know
how to consecrate my fields just like the

next guy in twenty-first century suburban
Van Nuys. And I know if I litter, or go faster

than I should, there will be consequences
and I'm okay with that and, and I want you all

to know that I would never litter and the
people who litter make me awfully mad

but we are all humans, and it is tough
out there to be a human, and sometimes

a piece of paper flies out of your hand
because of a wind, and you have no control

over the weather, so can't they keep that
in mind when they levy the fine, and is it

really necessary to have forty verses of
punishments when the wind can just

lift things out of your hands and you
can't do anything about it, I mean let's

just all be good. I want to be good.
I want to be good so bad. I don't need the

carrot on the stick or the promise of a
cookie or the threat of fleeing from no-one.

Let us grow strong from our desire to
be the *goodest* we can be.

Let us be so strong.
Let us be so strengthened.

במדבר
bamidbar

numbers

Bamidbar

This is the week everyone who counts is counted.
A lineage established so we know the results of
all the past and future begetting.

Somehow, despite these efforts, I'm missing a
few thousand years of direct links. I know who
my grandparents were, though I never met them.

And I have seen the names and even a picture
of one or two of the people who came before them.
And sometimes the word *Poland* is said or

White Russia (which is not as racist as it sounds).
I think I've even seen a picture of a boat ticket
and an electronic record of a street someone

once lived on in Bialystok. So I can get myself
back to Europe if I do the numbers backwards,
but once I'm there it stops. There is no *counting*.

I don't know which of my ancestors were responsible
for transporting the curtains and tapestries of the
Tabernacle. Perhaps none. As far as I know

we've never been in the curtains business.
I wonder how much money there is to be made
in curtains. I wonder which family flag those

who came before me planted in the desert.
And if it was to the north or south or any of the
other available directions spanning out from the

Numbers 1:1-4:20

temporary placement of the holiest of holies.
I know Moses camped to the east. There is
something incessant with our Jewish obsession

with the east. The east side of London, the east side
of Los Angeles. It took thirty years for me to be
embarrassed that I had moved so far west.

I need a new *Book of Numbers* that fills in the gaps.
From now on I'm counting everything and writing it all down.
A hundred thousand *Luperts* into the future and

they'll know exactly how many peaches were on
my tree. And how many fell to the ground inedible
because we're still paying for the Golden Calf.

I'm going to leave them a note. Mind the curtains.
It's at least a responsibility of people we knew.
And when you're feeling so very far away

remember, even your house has
an east side. You could get there
in a second.

Naso

They shall confess the sin they committed.

How much time have you got? And I thought it was
only the Catholics who confessed. Maybe they got it from us.
They've got the right idea with the ornately decorated wooden
booths with privacy windows. I think if I had a secret booth
I could say anything inside, or at least make it to Narnia.
It is good to put it all on the table, and to accept
the consequences for what you have put there.

May God bless you and watch over you.

Like a personal bodyguard, or a spiritual advisor, or
anyone who, at the end of a days worth of danger and traffic
and frustration will show me a list of everything I did
and then make the list disappear. The biggest brother
is watching with a fleet of sacred drones whose presence
we can only hope to sense. Please watch over me.
I can't read all the languages of all the signs, and
knowing You're there is sometimes all I have.

May God cause God's countenance to shine to you and favor you.

Or, as the kids say, can you please hook me up, oh Holy One.
I like to travel *first class* sometimes. I like when the chef chooses
my table for the unscheduled *amuse-bouche*. I like front-row center
seats, so, when You're favoring me, oh Kahuna with the mighty
countenance, I feel like I'm part of the action. Or, at the very least,
which often turns out to be the baseline most, when I do the things
I do every day, please make me feel like this is how it's supposed to be.
I want to land on top and, I want everyone there with me.
One vast plane of *top*, on a bed of Your favor –
      how it's supposed to be.

May God raise God's countenance toward you and grant you peace.

Yes, as long as You're looking at me and showing *me* favor can we throw in peace? Can You promise me that You're throwing in peace for everyone whether they show up for the Priestly Blessing or not. Can we do a universal blessing for everyone in every room on every piece of soil, where peace is automatic like oxygen? You don't have to think about it. It just enters into you like a biological imperative. This is the blessing I want, a granting of peace so universal we forget there was anything else. So raise Your Vulcan fingers to me, oh Holy One. I've never been more ready.

Behaalotecha

We've been in the shadow of this mountain for almost a year.
And now, with specific instructions (our history is never detailed
without specific instructions) we walk away

towards a place we once did not know, and now is
a vague memory. A place, that if you were to look at
on a map should only take a day or so to get to.

But this is the one task that doesn't come with
specific instructions. And so a generation of people
disappear into the desert, as we make our way

with *manna* raining out of the sky, because who doesn't
love a free meal? And apparently the answer is *us*
because the journey is arduous (it's so much easier

to sit at the base of a mountain than to follow a cloud
into the wilderness) and we won't take a step further
without meat. So Moses appeals to God, and God promises

meat will soon *come out of our noses,* which sounds like
a lot of meat, but, despite my vegetarianism, I don't even
want to eat a cucumber that came out of someone's nose.

But at least we know the suggestion box is working.
And on the way, after quail meat flies out of the sea for
us to gather up and eat, but not gluttonously because that

leads to death by plague, Moses decides to become celibate
which, honestly, is six or seven other poems worth of
discussion, but suffice it to say his sister, Miriam

isn't pleased, and complains, because that's what we do
in every situation, complain, and though the punishment
seems a strange match for the *crime,* she gets leprosy.

So, I guess, watch your tongues of dissatisfaction, and
enjoy whatever rains out of the sky for you to eat, as most
people don't have the benefit of *anything* they need

raining out of the sky, even *rain,* am I right Californians?
And let's cry for help for anyone with any affliction.
Like Moses did for his sister. The fewest words are

all we need. Please, God, heal her, or him, or them.
Make us whole as we march to the sound of Your trumpets
towards a land we'd like to know again.

Shelach

Just out of Egypt for a year or so and we already have
a system of espionage. Spies! Sent to the promised land.
An advance party to gather intelligence. Human Jewish
drones dwelling on the outskirts of Canaan.

For how long? Forty days of course. Forty is our default
unit of measure. There's no need to think about how much
time anything will take. It *will* be forty. And at the end of that
particular time period, the report comes back.

Most of our secret agents tell us *Large people! Impenetrable
walls!* They put a scare in the masses that Caleb and Joshua
couldn't assuage with a huge cluster of grapes, a pomegranate
and even a fig!

If only the purpose of spies was to gather fruit.
I would vote for that. Let's replace our secret organizations
with orchards. Our racial profiling with bags of produce.
Our extra screening with a field of grass.

This is the kind of secret information that would march me
forward instead of back to Egypt, to the comfort of slavery.
But the wind doesn't blow this way and we've failed another test.
It's all Moses can do to convince our Savior to not, once again,

wipe us all out. He's a vengeful one, the Holy One. And I
say *he* this time because I can't imagine a woman doing this. But
a flock of forward thinkers head to Canaan anyway and are killed.
The naysayer spies who focused on the difficulty

instead of the fruit, don't breathe another day.
And one man who gathers sticks on the Sabbath
is executed. You can see why the traditionally inclined
don't manipulate light switches on the Sabbath.

If the Holy One would wipe one person out just for
gathering sticks on a Saturday, better to sit in the dark.
So choose the grapes, my friends, the pomegranate
and the fig. It is produce that will lead you to the promised land.

The future is organic. Pesticide free. Grown locally.
Farm to Table. In your mouth. Our land of Canaan
a farmer's market. I'm feeling so bold, I may even
drive my car to get there on Saturday.

Korach

A rebellion against the establishment.
A dissenting family swallowed by the earth.
A sudden punitive plague eliminated by a man
wielding a staff that would soon sprout
almond blossoms.

Are you listening HBO? These are the plot points
of an epic trailer for a weekly series I'd love to watch
in the fall. Honestly, I'd love to watch now.
But the space between the announcement of
a production and its appearance in my digital world
makes me kvetch like two hundred fifty Israelites
in the desert who have nothing better to do.

(As a side note, if you could get Ian McShane
to play Korach, the rebel, I'll double the amount.
I'm paying you.)

And now that I think about it, it's not so much
of a side note. Oh the bad men McShane has played
on pay TV. Stealing our screens with an infectious
no good. Like a Korach, rebel *with* a cause,
challenging his first cousin Moses whose record,
so far, is pretty good if you consider we're
no longer in Egypt.

When the priests inside the tabernacle were
following the instructions for how to make their
holy garments, Korach was on the outskirts with
a pop up *Challenge Authority* t-shirt shop.

Except instead of "challenge" it was the ancient
Israelite teenage rebellious slang of the day.
He was the ultimate other side of the aisle
refusing to pass any useful legislation but
making darn sure his colleagues on the right
didn't either.

And what do we get for our youthful rebellions?
Most of us grow up, have children, watch them
question the same authority we are now a part of.
Almond blossoms in our closets, ready to pull out
to display our parlor tricks of wisdom. Doing
everything we can to prevent our young rebels
from being swallowed up by the earth.

I'm not usually the type to write a poem about
questioning authority and revolution. Outside of
an occasional strongly worded email to a
customer service department, I'm much more of
a *status-quo* kind of guy. But Korach, swallowed
inside the earth reminds me, we don't always
get our way...and that is our way.

Chukat

Oh water, source of life,
when I need you, I need you
which is all the time.

Oh water, you can't blame
Moses for striking the rock
instead of talking to it.

These days, and those days
if you talk to a rock, no one
will listen. Not even the rock.

Oh water, if you can get
the rock to listen, be kind.
Even the rock will grow

deaf ears if you issue
demands with fury. Surely
you're not angry with the rock?

It's not the rock's job to
give water anyway. Why
are you yelling at the rock?

Why are you hitting the rock?
What made you think the
rock would want to

develop any kind of flow?
Is this how you get what you
want? Is this how even

a rock should be treated?
Oh water, I need you like I
need you. I'm mostly you.

The best parts anyway.
Satisfying. Sustaining. Wet.
Is that redundant? Sorry,

wet is your best feature.
Oh water. Where am I going
with you? Rivers go where

they go and I'm just along
for the ride. Forty years in now
and there's the Jordan.

Oh water it's filled with you
and it won't be long before
we cross over. Most of us.

We're dropping like flies
in the desert. A sister, a brother
a generation of people who

remember Egypt's soil. Gone.
Oh water will you recognize us
when we get there?

We can almost taste the
land that was promised.
Sorry about the yelling.

Sorry about the stick.
We couldn't do this
without you.

Balak

Balaam (no relation) is hired to go to the Israelites
(every relation) and let curses fall out of his mouth.

On the way his donkey (of the famous Moabite donkeys)
stops because only she can see the angel blocking the road.

Balaam (loves his coffee) strikes the donkey
who, like something out of Narnia (not Jewish), begins

to admonish him in the language of the day. Balaam
(a sorcerer, a wizard) displays no issue with

a talking donkey and simply engages in conversation.
Everyone's eyes are now open – Balaam (two eyes)

Donkey (two more eyes) and the angel (number of
eyes angels are known to have.) Now (not before)

Balaam is the sort to have awareness of the
presence of angels. (Are you? You should be. They're

right there.) The journey continues (we should all
be so lucky.) And three times upon encountering

the Israelites, Balaam (glutton, foreigner) who
was hired to say curses, to damage with words,

can only say blessings. *To Hell with you* becomes
How lovely are your tents? – *May the fleas of*

a thousand camels infest your armpits becomes
Your dwelling places, oh Israel, extend like streams

Numbers 22:2-25:9

like gardens by the river, like aloe which God planted
like cedars by the water. It's poetry. It's beautiful

poetry. (Do you like poetry?) And now we say these
words every morning (or just on Saturday mornings

or maybe you say different words or maybe you
just think them). May this forever be your way

with words. If curses and hateful speech are
ready to fall out of your mouth, let them turn to

blessings. Your intended *cursee* may be *the one.*
Keep your eyes open for angels on the road.

And pay attention to the behaviors of the animals
you co-habit with. (dogs, cats, donkeys, fish,

children) They often see things before you do.
The gutters falling off your house. The moment

before the earth shakes plates out of your cabinets.
How lovely are your tents, (who still lives in a tent?)

oh, citizens of earth, your dwelling places, (house,
apartment, kibbutz, micro-space, man-cave, commune)

oh, human animal, oh, gentle ears, oh, stranger on the
road, oh family, oh, blessings to you. Never curses.

Pinchas

It's always nice to see a project through to the end. Especially one you've been working on for forty years, a lifetime really, though back then people either lived much longer or they were prematurely smitten for lying with a Midianite.

So when Moses who's been working on this project, this project of getting all the people into the promised land, who's been working on this project since back in the days when the Lord was just a glint of fire on a bush, halfway up another mountain...

So when Moses, who already knows he's not going to see this through to the end because of a brief transgression with a rock and a stick...

So when Moses is asked to climb to the top of a mountain, Mount Abrim if you really must know, the mountain across Jordan...When Moses is asked to stand on top of this mountain and view the promised land, the culmination of his life's work, a distant soil his shoes will never know...

it must have been...well you can imagine. You've probably been there. If you've ever experienced anything unrequited you know exactly how Moses must have felt. Moses, the star of books two through five, turned lame duck leader, asked to pass his spiritual power onto Joshua the rookie.

The end is in sight and it's not the land he sees from the top of this mountain. These old bones will rest in Moab. But don't let me skip ahead. We've still got a whole book to go and it's the longest one. Heck, there are still two chapters left in this one.

You can't blame me. I get nostalgic about things that haven't happened yet. More often than not the present moment escapes me as I worry about its passing.
How many of us exist perpetually on our own Mount Abrims pining for the distant vista, completely missing the glorious view?

This is the curse of the thoughtful human, the task-focused. We, temporary mammals, this Earth not ours, but meant for the next, and, when it comes down to it, not them either. Unbreakable cycle. Know this – the promised land is where your feet are right now. Where this air enters your nose. Concentrate on that breath and you will never be left alone on a mountain.

Matot-Massei

I like to think of Israel as a promised land
a refuge, a holy place where everyone in
my extended family belongs.

But how many Midianites did we have
to kill before we got there? Every time I
see the word *conquer* in our

Holy Text, and it's us who's doing the
conquering, I get the discomfort of
a boy whose first entire decade

was the seventies, on the back of the
generation of peace and love, so fresh,
flowers weren't even retro yet.

To say it was a different time doesn't
quite cover it. Back in the millennia where
two camels were the family sedan

you couldn't simply trot up your herd
to a new neighborhood and ask the
residents if they minded if you

set up your tents over there.
The answer might come in blood
yours or theirs, and in the end

you or them were no longer.
What is it with a promised land that
leads to the death of so many?

I'd like to say it's all fiction but
it seems we're still conquering
the same neighborhoods.

We're still having conversations
about who gets what piece of land
without much consideration of

who's occupying that space now.
Tell me God, Tell me Moses, in your
conversations about who gets to go where

is this what you had in mind?
I dream of a future where the only
lines people have to consider are

the ones on pieces of paper where
they write their poetry. I was born in
the age of free love and I never

quite got over it. This is my promised land.
This is the land that will make us strong. This
is the land that will make us strengthened.

דברים
devarim

deuteronomy

Devarim

Have you ever started a new book, the last in a series you've been reading for a while? You're invested and

this is the beginning of your final time in that world. Well here we are at the beginning of the fifth of five.

It opens like a story arced TV show. *Previously in the Torah* as Moses recounts everything that led to this

moment. There's veiled scolding for transgressions. We recount the time Moses said, thirty-nine years ago

when the people were first at the foot of the promised land, *I'll turn this Exodus right around*. And he made

good on that promise. The family vacation was cancelled and we realize, these decades later, those

people whose feet touched Egyptian soil, are not the same people who will cross the Jordan. How's that

for follow-through parenting? Oh, Moses I love, as a poet, that this book, this chapter, this *parsha* is called

Words, and that you'll spend most of it saying them. I am a person of the words just as we are a people

of the Books that contain them. This oral history your final classroom, reads like a spoken word event.

Did the Israelites snap when you showed how God multiplied them? *You are today as many as there*

are stars in the heavens. We've got a population
explosion on our hands and that's a promise kept

if I've ever seen one. I know I would have snapped
at every pause out of habit. Or maybe I did. I keep

forgetting I was there. I could describe what I was
wearing, but mundane details aren't what this is about.

Watch out Canaanites! As soon as Moses gets done
with this piece, we're coming for you, or at least

the land you sit in. That's our other promise.
I'm going to read this book slow. Not more than one

chapter a week. I have a feeling when it's all over
I'm going to start the whole series again.

Va'etchanan

This is the story Moses tells:
In a last ditch effort, he pleads with God
Let me into the Promised Land.
The response comes: *Go tell it to the mountain,*
Moses. You'll get a lovely view, but that's
as far as we're taking this.

It's a recent event, this conversation, but Moses
is a reminiscer. I can't blame him. I get nostalgic
about things that haven't happened yet.
Have I already told you that? That's okay.
I don't mean to make an excuse, but so much
of this book is telling what has already been told.

We're only in chapter two and it feels like a
clip show. Are the writers on vacation?
I remember always feeling cheated when
a new episode came on and it was just the
regular players sitting on a couch flashing back
to footage I'd already seen. Does this really count?

Or do I need to hear this again? Do we all
need to hear this again. Remember what happened
with the idol? We have such a short memory.
And those with the shortest memories
aren't here any more.

Listen Israel: God, who I've mentioned before
is your God. And you can count the number of
Gods we have on one finger.

Deuteronomy 3:23-7:11

That's the most important thing we have to say,
so it's being said again. That's the most important
thing we have to say, so here's a list of instructions
about what to do with those words.

Got a door? Put it there. Got a forehead? Put it there.
Hands? You guessed it. Gates? That should go
without saying. Children? Right in their heads, please.
Write this down so you don't forget it. Put it everywhere.
You won't have Moses nagging you like a parent
for very much longer. He's on his death speech.
Soon, he'll only be talking to a mountain. Soon,
he'll just be a rumor.

This is the generation who knew God's presence.
Who were so scared of It they asked only Moses to
interact with It.

Now we only know stories of the mountain.
Of the man who died on the mountain.
Of a Presence we've been looking for
ever since.

Eikev

Because we're coming to the end of a history that's not provable.
Because we only get to enter this land because it was promised

to our fore-parents and not because we deserve it. Because of the
long list of reasons why we don't deserve it. The complaining, the

calf. Did you know *that* calf was ground to golden dust and tossed
into a brook? Because our mistake became a gold-rush for future

middle-easterners. Because of all that. Because we're so used to
manna raining out of the sky and now we'll need to learn to find

food in a conventional manner. Because milk and honey are meant
to flow together. Try it one night – heated up in a pot, poured in your

favorite mug, then down your throat. Because of that comfort.
Because these words I teach to my children I sometimes take literally,

and can only think of a new neighborhood where milk comes out of
the faucets and the rivers are nothing but honey, and I don't know

how I'd navigate that, and the unwanted attention from bears.
Because we should love our neighbors as ourselves and welcome

the stranger into our tent, except for the Canaanites, of course, who
we are about to slaughter and whose idols we will crush to more

golden dust, and maybe someone will benefit from the gold of their
history. Because if we abandon the precepts which have been

laid out for us, and which have been repeated over and over, and
are even now being repeated by a man who is scared, almost to

his death, that we'll screw it up. Because, we're told, screwing it up will lead to our exile. And isn't it funny that I'm writing this from a

foreign land where I've spent my whole life, where everyone I know acts like they are not a stranger. Because my visits to the promised

land are just visits. Because of all that. Because I want to deserve a promised land like it was assumed the first ones of my kind did.

Because I want the milk and honey in my cup to be a just reward, a promise worth keeping, a gold rush in my mouth.

Re'eh

Welcome back to the longest orientation meeting
in the history of orientation meetings. I hope someone
is writing all this down, because he is still talking.

He is still telling us about all the things we've
already done, and all the things we should make sure
to do, and the very fine points about how we should

go about doing them. You'll never have to guess
how much of your fruit should go to the poor every
seventh year, or how much of your fruit you should

bring to Jerusalem and only eat in Jerusalem,
and if you're concerned that transporting a lot of
fruit to Jerusalem is going to be an issue, not to

worry, there's a backup plan where you can sell your
fruit locally, which the restaurants love putting on their
menus. *We only serve locally sourced produce,* they'll say

and you'll go there, and pay extra because it feels good to
read that, and you'll use the proceeds of your locally grown
and locally sold fruit to buy food in Jerusalem, and then

you'll eat that food in Jerusalem, and then, according
to this text, which *is* being written down, you're good,
you're covered so, I wouldn't worry about it.

What I might worry about, though, is the choice between
two mountains, Gerizim and Ebal. Because, half of us
are going up one, and the other half the other.

Half of us will say a blessing and the other half a curse.
And we'll be reminded that it's always one or the other
and which one it is, is often a direct result of the

choices we make. And we have been making this decision,
this same decision, since we built a golden calf, since we
stole our brother's birthright, since another brother

killed another brother, since the forbidden fruit went
into our mouths, since, essentially, forever. So make sure
you climb up the right mountain, lest you get kicked

out of the garden again, or burst into flames again
(it's been known to happen, check the earlier chapters).
Since everything from your first breath to your last

is about this choice, this red pill or blue pill, this fork in
the road, this Gerizim or Ebal. *Behold,* your promised land
is a *yes* or *no* away. The other side of the river is coming.

Shoftim

A septuplet of haiku

I
Worship an idol
be put to death. These are the
laws of our people.

II
A king shall write two
Torah scrolls in his life. No
mention of a queen.

III
Priests get no land, but
unlimited free meat and, God
their inheritance.

IV
No sorcerers or
mediums. in other words:
No Coney Islands.

V
Only the prophets
speak for God. The murderers
get their own cities.

VI
Let's all build houses
and get married. Then no-one
has to go to war.

VII
May I suggest we
treat all people like we're told
to treat their fruit trees.

Ki Teitzei

If you are at war and find
your captives are beautiful

the laws of our people,
seventy four of which are

listed this week, tell you
this could lead to a

bonafide engagement.
If you are at war and you

find your captives are
beautiful, how does that

make you feel about
having taken them captive?

If you are at war and find
your captives are beautiful

who has captured whom?
If you are at war and find

your captives are beautiful
do you forget what it is

the war was about?
Do you forget the meaning

of the word *war?* Do you
get in the cage with your

captives and lose yourself
in their beauty?

If you are at war and find
your captives are beautiful

you may take them home.
That is allowed, according

to the words we read this
week, and every time this

week comes along in the
years past, and the ones

which will pass. You may
find, after a time, your

beautiful captives, in your
home, may not find you

the way you find them, and
after a time, you will have

to let them go to wherever
it is they wish to go.

That is the law. That is
the sacred word on

the beautiful, who you've
captured. (Did you see

they were beautiful before
or after you captured them?)

Let them go. They will not
sing in your cage, these birds

of war, these human birds,
these spoils of war who

will not spoil, these captives.
You know what to do.

Ki Tavo

It's not going to be easy crossing that river
and the rule book keeps getting longer
and we're going to have to climb mountains
and shout everything we've done good and bad
and if that's not enough, there's going to be labor,
stones to carve and coat with lime, when we'd
all rather use the lime to coat our mojito glasses,
and we're going to have to bring our first fruits
to the Temple so the priests have fruits, when
we'd much rather eat our first fruits that we
planted and grew with our own free hands
and the first Temple isn't going to build itself
and we'll have to *slaughter peace offerings*
and wonder how the words *slaughter* and
peace ever got to be in the same sentence,
did they meet at an interfaith event and
hit it off, and there's a commitment here
because we were chosen, and we agreed
to choose, and if we're thinking of running
away at the altar, or the river, there's a long
list of curses for that, I mean anything you
might do that slightly strays from the pack
and there's a curse for that, and a curse for
this, and consequences, we really get into
the consequences so unless you want your
children to be captives, and cicadas to eat
everything you grow, and to never drink wine
and to have your corpse eaten by birds,
you'd better consider walking the difficult
path, the righteous path, the path cross the
river, the path up whichever mountain your
tribe has been assigned to go up, and build

Deuteronomy 26:1-29:8

the altar, and bring the fruits, and be a standup guy, or standup girl if that's how ya go, because now we have the heart to know what is right is right, and we have the eyes to see we did the right thing leaving the narrow place, and we have the ears to hear the melodies of freedom we've been hearing for forty years while we've worn the same shirt and shoes every day, that whole time, and they have never worn out, and still smell as fresh as they did the day we got them from the store, and I'm not sure we even had stores back in Egypt, and maybe after we set up the Holy Temple, and get all squared away with the distribution of our first fruits, we can build a shopping center, nothing big, just a mini mall, or maybe even a strip mall with two or three stores, because we deserve it and by God, and I really mean, by *God*, it's a miracle!

Nitzavim

This is for you.
You standing at the mountain
and you who only read about the mountain
in a book.

This is for you, all of you.
Your leaders, your elders, your elected officials,
your men and women, your whatever you
decide you are.

This is for you.
Your children, and their children and their
children. We could go on forever like that.
Let's do that. Let's go on forever.

This is for you.
Your woodcutters, your people who make
the water come out of the spigots. Your
haircutters, your hair weavers. Your
people who lost all their hair
long ago.

This is for you.
Your food preparers, your internet mavens,
your long dead, still cleaning the sand
out of their sandals.

This is for you.
Your believers, your boat drivers, your
cantors, and cops, your cat lovers, your
hungry, your fat.

This is for you.
The ones who vehemently deny this
is for you, it is *especially* for you.
It is double for you.

It is already yours.
It is already spilling out of your pockets
your reusable grocery bags, your
untamed closets.

So clean some space off a shelf, or
better, build a whole new wall of shelves
This thing that is yours, takes up
a lot of space.

So make that space.
So choose life, when given the choice,
and assume you're always being given
that choice, and live, and really live.

This is for you.
This is yours.
Take it.

Vayelech

Moses at one hundred and twenty one years
feels he can no longer come and go, and so
he will stay while every one else goes.

Me at one hundred and twenty one years
feels like I should have stopped coming and
going for at least fifty of them.

Moses at one hundred and twenty one years
still manages to jot down an entire Torah
for safe keeping.

Me at one hundred and twenty one years
will spend my entire last day dotting a single "i".

Moses at one hundred and twenty one years
commingles with the very presence of the Holy
One, blessed be (S)He.

Me at one hundred and twenty one years
still claiming intellectual disbelief, but plea for
one more day when no-one's looking.

Moses at one hundred and twenty one years
composes an entire song meant to guide a nation
for generations after his bones are known.

Me at one hundred and twenty one years
still resting on the laurels of that one good thing
I did when I was thirty-five.

Moses at one hundred and twenty one years
issues commands like a governor in his prime.

Me at one hundred and twenty one years
knows better than to tell anyone what to do.

Moses at one hundred twenty one years
has had a pretty good run and doesn't plan on
slowing down. Just stopping.

Me at one hundred and twenty one years
pleading, *don't hide Your face from me.* Just show
me a pillar of smoke. I'll believe.

Ha'azinu

I've always said go out with a song.
Let it be the last taste in their mouth
the culmination of the experience.

This one's a little bit wordy but
so are some of the epics of Bob Dylan
and he just won a Nobel Prize

so what do I know?
If you've been reading, you know the
answer to that is *very little*.

I'm going to have to read this
whole thing again. I'm going to have
to memorize the words to this

song, figure out how to play it on guitar
so I can teach it to the Jewish ears of
the San Fernando Valley.

Maybe not the whole thing
at once. Just a little bit every week.
I'll put the words in front of them.

No-one has to know it by heart.
They just have to sing it. The verses
of our triumphs and transgressions.

The stories of everyone who came
before us. The ones we name our
children after. The ones whose

names our American mouths
could never properly pronounce.
This is our song.

Our story and anthem.
Our melody which, now that I
think of it, I *have* been singing

bits and pieces of since the
moment I wandered into that
first room with my guitar.

I finally know what I've been
entrusted with. I'm going to keep
doing this until it's my turn

to wander up the mountain
and get a glimpse of the future
I'll never know.

I'm putting this track on auto-repeat.
These days, no-one has heard of the
rewind button. But rest assured.

We're going to hear this again.

Vezot Hab'rachah

You've had this experience.
The bookmark is as close to the end
as possible. You want to savor every word
before the last page is turned.

This is pure denouement.
All the action has happened and the
main players are behaving with a nostalgia
that encompasses all history.

Our first family appears in chapter
after chapter. Ghosts we thought we wouldn't
hear from again receive their blessings.
This is the culmination of so much begetting.

And our main guy, touched by the face of
Our Main Guy, has the final word, and
disappears up the final mountain.
Can you imagine how many times I've

used the word *mountain* in these poems?
There are certain resources which will
tell you how many times any word was
used in a TV show or the Torah.

Repetition is a great tradition, and
when you start this whole thing over
you'd better do it from the top of a mountain.
We are the lucky ones who don't just

get a view of the promised land from,
get ready for it, *the mountain*. But we
get to buy airplane tickets, or take the
long walk and put our feet on that promise.

Like an old friend, God buries Moses.
The exact location never revealed, to avoid
a Jim Morrison in Père Lachaise situation.
Do you find that image too funny for

this ending? Let us not forget who we are.
The bookmark is on the table. The last
page is turned only to reveal we have
turned to where we started.

*In the beginning of God's creation of the
heavens and the earth*...This isn't the first time
you've seen those words. And it
won't be the last.

The author preparing to teach Torah through song.

About The Author

Two-time Pushcart Prize, and Best of the Net nominee Rick Lupert has been involved in the Los Angeles poetry community since 1990. He was awarded the Beyond Baroque Distinguished Service Award in 2014 for service to the Los Angeles poetry community. He served for two years as a co-director of the non-profit literary organization Valley Contemporary Poets. His poetry has appeared in numerous magazines and literary journals, including *The Los Angeles Times, Rattle, Chiron Review, Red Fez, Zuzu's Petals, Stirring, The Bicycle Review, Caffeine Magazine, Blue Satellite* and others. He edited the anthologies *Ekphrastia Gone Wild - Poems Inspired by Art, A Poet's Haggadah: Passover through the Eyes of Poets*, and *The Night Goes on All Night - Noir Inspired Poetry*, and is the author of twenty one other books: *Beautiful Mistakes, Donut Famine, Romancing the Blarney Stone, Making Love to the 50 Ft. Woman, The Gettysburg Undress* (Rothco Press), *Nothing in New England is New, Death of a Mauve Bat, Sinzibuckwud!, We Put Things In Our Mouths, Paris: It's The Cheese, I Am My Own Orange County, Mowing Fargo, I'm a Jew. Are You?, Feeding Holy Cats, Stolen Mummies, I'd Like to Bake Your Goods, A Man With No Teeth Serves Us Breakfast* (Ain't Got No Press), *Lizard King of the Laundromat, Brendan Constantine is My Kind of Town* (Inevitable Press) and *Up Liberty's Skirt* (Cassowary Press), and the spoken word album "Rick Lupert Live and Dead" (Ain't Got No Press). He hosted the long running Cobalt Café reading series in Canoga Park for almost twenty-one years and has read his poetry all over the world.

Rick created and maintains Poetry Super Highway, an online resource and publication for poets (PoetrySuperHighway.com), Haikuniverse, a daily online small poem publication (Haikuniverse.com), and writes and occasionally draws the daily web comic *Cat and Banana* with Brendan Constantine. (facebook.com/catandbanana) He also writes the weekly Jewish poetry blog *From the Lupertverse* for JewishJournal.com

Currently Rick works as a music teacher at synagogues in Southern California and as a graphic and web designer for anyone who would like to help pay his mortgage.

Rick's Other Books and Recordings

Beautiful Mistakes
Rothco Press ~ May, 2018

17 Holy Syllables
Ain't Got No Press ~ January, 2018

A Poet's Siddur: Friday Evening (edited by)
Ain't Got No Press ~ November, 2017

Donut Famine
Rothco Press ~ December, 2016

Romancing the Blarney Stone
Rothco Press ~ December, 2016

Professor Clown on Parade
Rothco Press ~ December, 2016

Rick Lupert Live and Dead (Album)
Ain't Got No Press ~ March, 2016

Making Love to the 50 Ft. Woman
Rothco Press ~ May, 2015

The Gettysburg Undress
Rothco Press ~ May, 2014

Ekphrastia Gone Wild (edited by)
Ain't Got No Press ~ July, 2013

Nothing in New England is New
Ain't Got No Press ~ March, 2013

Death of a Mauve Bat
Ain't Got No Press ~ January, 2012

The Night Goes On All Night Noir Inspired Poetry (edited by)
Ain't Got No Press ~ November, 2011

Sinzibuckwud!
Ain't Got No Press ~ January, 2011

We Put Things In Our Mouths
Ain't Got No Press ~ January, 2010

A Poet's Haggadah (edited by)
Ain't Got No Press ~ April, 2008

A Man With No Teeth Serves Us Breakfast
Ain't Got No Press ~ May, 2007

I'd Like to Bake Your Goods
Ain't Got No Press ~ January, 2006

Stolen Mummies
Ain't Got No Press ~ February, 2003

Brendan Constantine is My Kind of Town
Inevitable Press ~ September, 2001

Up Liberty's Skirt
Cassowary Press ~ March, 2001

Feeding Holy Cats
Cassowary Press ~ May, 2000

I'm a Jew, Are You?
Cassowary Press ~ May, 2000

Mowing Fargo
Sacred Beverage Press ~ December, 1998

Lizard King of the Laundromat
The Inevitable Press ~ February, 1998

I Am My Own Orange County
Ain't Got No Press ~ May, 1997

Paris: It's The Cheese
Ain't Got No Press ~ May, 1996

For more information:
www.PoetrySuperHighway.com

www.ingramcontent.com/pod-product-compliance
Lightning Source LLC
Chambersburg PA
CBHW052026290426
44112CB00014B/2394